A Special Gift for

_____

From

_____

Date

_____

Dedication

This book is dedicated to an
early experience with our Lord Jesus Christ
for all its young readers and to my four
grandchildren: Regan, Ryan,
Sasha, and Sean.

My First Christian

ABC BOOK

Bryant C. Buck

My First Christian ABC Book
by Bryant C. Buck
Copyright ©2009

ISBN 978-1-58169-3225
For Worldwide Distribution
Printed in the U.S.A.

Evergreen Press
P.O. Box 191540 • Mobile, AL 36619
800-367-8203
www.evergreenpress.com

Acknowledgments

I wish to thank my wife, Emily,
and my good friend Judith Fruin for all
their input into the making of this book.
To both of you I say, like the cartoon
character Dora, "I couldn't have
done it without you."

A is for ask–
we request from above.

B is for Bible,
God's Word written in love.

C is for Christ,
who died on the cross.

D is for David,
just one stone he did toss.

E is for Earth
where God's life we receive.

F is for faith,

so we trust and believe.

G is for grace
and His mercy well known.

H is for heaven—
the seat of God's throne.

I is for Israel,
the people God chose.

J is for Jesus,
from the grave He arose.

K is for kindness,
which we show to others.

L is for love

for our sisters and brothers.

M is for Moses,
from Yahweh he heard.

N is for Noah,

who built the ark by God's Word.

O is for olives,
the fruit and the trees.

P is for prayer,
which we do on our knees.

Q is for quiet time,
when we hear from the Lord.

R is for resurrection, over death Jesus soared!

S is for salvation,
which Christ gives us from sin.

T is for temple,
but *our* temple's within.

U is for unity—
we're together in God.

V is for victory,
over evil we trod.

W is for worship,
when we praise and we sing.

X is for eXult
in the joy of our King.

יֵשׁוּעַ

Y is for Yeshua,
Jesus' original name.

Z is for zeal,
for God's glory and fame.

To the Parents...

It's never too early in life to learn about Jesus and the Christian faith. The Bible teaches us that Jesus is the author and finisher of our faith. May Jesus be the author of your child's faith from an early age!